A Book
By ME,

_____

(name)

Myself

MY Book about CHRISTMAS

By **ME,**
Myself

I wrote it!
I drew it!

with a little help from
THE **GRINCH** &

Dr. Seuss

Random House New York

TM & copyright © by Dr. Seuss Enterprises, L.P. 2016

All rights reserved. Published in the United States by Random House Children's Books, a division of Penguin Random House LLC, New York. Adapted from *How the Grinch Stole Christmas* TM & copyright © by Dr. Seuss Enterprises, L.P. 1957, copyright renewed 1985.

Random House and the colophon are registered trademarks of Penguin Random House LLC.

Visit us on the Web!
Seussville.com
randomhousekids.com

Educators and librarians, for a variety of teaching tools, visit us at RHTeachersLibrarians.com

ISBN 978-0-553-52446-8

Library of Congress Control Number: 2016943950

Printed in the United States of America

10 9 8 7 6 5 4 3 2 1

MY BOOK about CHRISTMAS

Every *Who*
Down in *Who*-ville
Liked Christmas a lot . . .

I like **Christmas:**

- ☐ a lot

- ☐ more than my birthday

- ☐ more than ICE CREAM

- ☐ more than _____

But the Grinch,
Who lived just
north of *Who*-ville,
Did NOT!

How I FEEL about the Grinch:

I think he's funny. ☐

I think he's scary. ☐

I think he's sad. ☐

I like him! ☐

_____ ☐

Every *Who* hangs a stocking
and a mistletoe wreath.

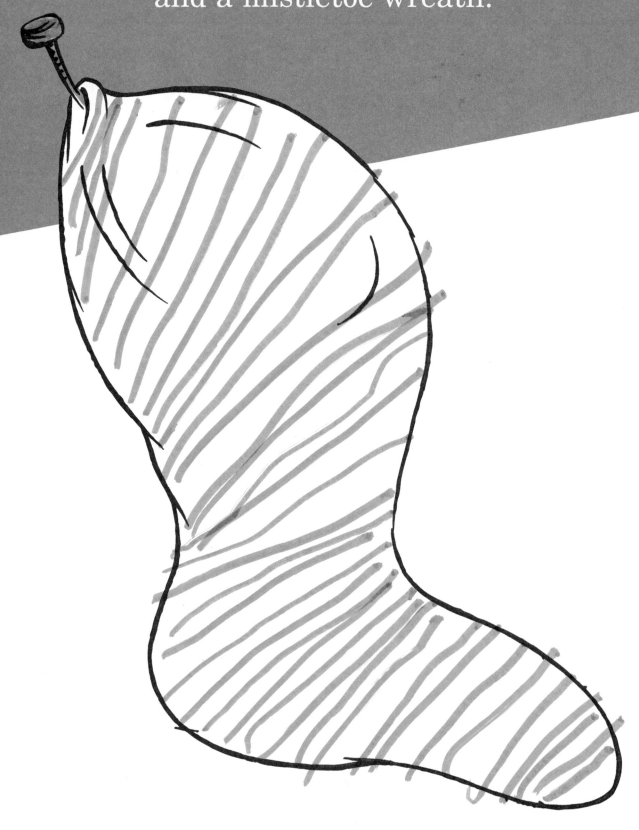

My stocking looks like this

I decorated this wreath ↑

My family gets ready for Christmas by doing these things:

(circle all the things you do)

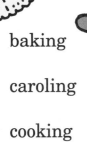
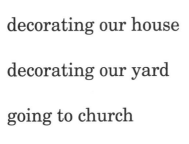

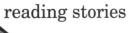
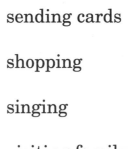

baking

caroling

cooking

crafting

decorating our house

decorating our yard

going to church

hanging stockings

hanging wreaths

making presents

reading stories

sending cards

shopping

singing

visiting family

visiting friends

volunteering

watching movies

_____

_____

My family has a Christmas tree.

- [ ] Always
  - [ ] We cut it down ourselves.
  - [ ] We buy it.
  - [ ] We build it from a box.
  - [ ] We _____.
- [ ] Sometimes
  - [ ] We _____.
- [ ] Never
  - [ ] We _____.

We decorate our tree with:

(circle what you use)

bows

candles

candy canes

cookies

cranberries

fake snow

flowers

garland

homemade ornaments

only colored lights

only white lights

white AND colored lights

paper chains

paper snowflakes

pinecones

popcorn

seashells

shiny ornaments

tinsel

(I place it on the tree.)

(I THROW it on the tree!)

_____

_____

_____

This is my tree when it is done

Here's a drawing of my **favorite** ornament:

I like it **BEST** because:

_____

_____

On top of our tree, we put a:

star

angel

snowflake

baked potato

_____

It looks like this ↘

On Christmas morning . . .

All the *Who* girls and boys
Would wake bright and early.
They'd rush for their toys!

I hope Santa brings me

these presents:

1. _____

2. _____

3. _____

**I wrote this letter to Santa
about all the good things I've done.**

Dear Santa,

_____

_____

_____

_____

_____

_____

Love,

your friend _____

And *then!* Oh, the noise!
Oh, the Noise! Noise! Noise! Noise!
That's *one* thing he hated.
The NOISE! NOISE! NOISE! NOISE!

Help the Grinch get back to his quiet cave!

START

FINISH

Then the *Whos*, young and old,
would sit down to a feast.
They would feast on *Who*-pudding,
and rare *Who*-roast-beast.

We have these at MY family's feast:

(circle what you eat)

apple pie	biscuits and gravy	curry
baba ghanoush	bûche de Noël	dim sum
bagels	candied yams	duck
baklava	cheese	dumplings
beef	cheesecake	egg rolls
	chestnuts	eggs
	chicken	falafel
	chili	fish
	chowder	fish-and-chips
	chow mein	fondue
	clams	French fries
	cookies	fruitcake
	crepes	gingerbread

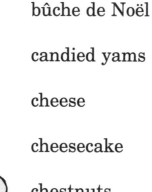

goat	panettone	stuffing
goose	pasta	tabbouleh
grits	pfeffernüsse	tacos
ham	pie	takeout
hamburgers	pierogies	tamales
hummus	pizza	tempeh
ice cream	plums	tofu
lamb	popcorn	turkey
lasagna	pork	venison
latkes	pumpkin pie	vindaloo
lebkuchen	quesadillas	waffles
liver	rice and beans	*Who*-hash
lobster	roast beast	*Who*-pudding
macaroni and cheese	salad	NONE of the above!
mashed potatoes	sandwiches	We eat:
meat loaf	sausage	_____
moose	seitan	My FAVORITE is:
noodles	soup	_____
oysters	spanakopita	But don't give me any:
pancakes	stollen	_____

It's a **tradition!**
Every Christmas, we eat

_____ .

This is what it looks like ↘

I asked for the **recipe.**
Here it is:

Recipe: _____

Ingredients: _____

_____

Instructions: _____

_____

_____

_____

_____

And **THEN** they'd do something
He liked least of all!
Every *Who* down in *Who*-ville,
the tall and the small,

These are my **favorite**
Christmas songs:

_____

_____

_____

_____

Would stand close together,
with Christmas bells ringing.
They'd stand hand-in-hand.
And the *Whos* would start singing!

I like to **sing** in these places:

☐ around the Christmas tree

☐ at church

☐ at home

☐ at school

☐ in the bathtub

☐ _____

☐ I don't really like to sing.

The Grinch wanted to stop Christmas from coming. But *how*?

Then he got an idea— THE GRINCH GOT A WONDERFUL, AWFUL IDEA!

He was going to *STEAL* Christmas!

Trying to steal Christmas is . . .

a wonderful idea ☐

an awful idea ☐

a wonderful, awful idea ☐

Giving someone a present because *you* really want to play with it is . . .

a wonderful idea ☐

an awful idea ☐

a wonderful, awful idea ☐

Eating candy for Christmas dinner is . . .

a wonderful idea ☐

an awful idea ☐

a wonderful, awful idea ☐

Staying up late to see Santa arrive is . . .

a wonderful idea ☐

an awful idea ☐

a wonderful, awful idea ☐

"I know *just* what to do!"
The Grinch laughed in his throat.
And he made a quick
Santy Claus hat and a coat.

I've seen Santa Claus:

at the North Pole ☐

in a parade ☐

at a store ☐

at my house ☐

at the mall ☐

on a rooftop ☐

on the street ☐

on TV ☐

_____ ☐

This is ME with Santa ↘

paste your picture here

The Grinch couldn't find a reindeer.
So he made one instead.

I have a pet.

YES ☐ NO ☐

My pet's name is

_____ .

My pet would . . .

wear a horn on its head ☐

rather chew on a horn ☐

I dress up my pet for Christmas.

YES ☐ NO ☐

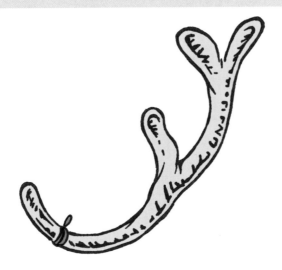

If my pet wore a horn on its head, my pet would look like this ➤

Then the Grinch said, "Giddap!"
And the sleigh started down

START

Help Max find the way to *Who*-ville!

Toward the homes where the *Whos* Lay a-snooze in their town.

FINISH

All their windows were dark.
Quiet snow filled the air.
All the *Whos* were all dreaming
sweet dreams without care.

It **snows** where I live.

Sometimes ☐

Never ☐

All the time! Snow! Snow! SNOW! ☐

I drew this snowman

The Grinch came to the first house and slid down the chimney.

Santa gets into MY house by . . .

climbing down the chimney ☐

using a magic key ☐

pressing the buzzer ☐

teleporting from the North Pole ☐

I leave **Santa** . . .

cookies and milk ☐

celery and carrots ☐

a nice note ☐

_____ ☐

He took every present!
Then he did the *same* thing
at the *other Whos'* houses!

If the Grinch took all MY presents . . .

I'd cry BOO-HOO! ☐

I wouldn't LIKE it,

but I'd be okay.

It's Christmas, after all! ☐

The **BEST** present I ever got was:

_____

It was the **BEST** because:

_____

_____

I make presents.

YES ☐   NO ☐
check one

I buy presents.

YES ☐   NO ☐
check one

I make some presents and buy others.

YES ☐   NO ☐
check one

This year, 20_____,
I am giving these presents:

A _____ to _____

A _____ to _____

A _____ to _____

A _____ to _____

The Grinch packed up his sled.

Packed it up with their presents!
The ribbons! The wrappings!
The tags! And the tinsel!
The trimmings! The trappings!

When it's time to **wrap** presents . . .

I use printed wrapping paper. ☐

I use paper I decorate myself. ☐

I use lots of ribbons and bows. ☐

I use LOTS of tape. ☐

I use gift bags. ☐

I'm better at OPENING presents

than wrapping them. ☐

Three thousand feet up!
Up the side of Mt. Crumpit,
He rode with his load
to the tiptop to dump it!

"They're just waking up!
I know *just* what they'll do!
The *Whos* down in *Who*-ville
will all cry BOO-HOO!"

On Christmas morning,

I wake up . . .

REALLY early (I hardly sleep) ☐

early ☐

normal time ☐

late ☐

My parents wake up . . . .

early—they're as excited as I am! ☐

when I crash into their bedroom ☐

late—it makes me crazy! ☐

"That's a noise," grinned the Grinch,
"That I simply MUST hear!"
So he paused.
And the Grinch put his hand to his ear.

Things I **like to hear**
on Christmas:

Christmas carols ☐

church bells ☐

laughter ☐

my family and friends saying "I love you" ☐

people saying "Merry Christmas!" ☐

_____ ☐

_____ ☐

Things I *don't* like to hear on Christmas (or any other day)!

car horns honking ☐

crying ☐

fingernails on a blackboard ☐

glass breaking ☐

that I have to go to bed ☐

_____ ☐

_____ ☐

But the sound the Grinch heard
wasn't *sad*. It was *merry*!

**Every *Who* down in *Who*-ville,
the tall and the small,
Was singing!
Without any presents at all!**

Things that make ME so happy
I could burst into song:

_____

_____

**He HADN'T stopped
Christmas from coming!
IT CAME! Somehow or other,
it came just the same!**

Christmas means these things to me:

caring ☐

faith ☐

family ☐

friends ☐

giving ☐

happiness ☐

helping ☐

"Maybe Christmas," he thought,
"*doesn't* come from a store.
Maybe Christmas . . . perhaps . . .
means a little bit more!"

joy ☐

love ☐

no school ☐

sharing ☐

snow ☐

_____ ☐

_____ ☐

Well . . . in *Who*-ville they say
That the Grinch's small heart
Grew three sizes that day!

I have GROWN my own heart by doing these good deeds:

1. _____

_____

2. _____

_____

3. _____

_____

4. _____

_____

**The Grinch brought back the toys
and the food for the feast . . .**

And he . . . HE HIMSELF . . . !
The Grinch carved the roast beast!

The Grinch celebrates Christmas with the *Whos*.
I celebrate Christmas with these people:

I asked my family and friends
to write down what makes
THEIR hearts grow at Christmas.

I think they are as smart and wise as the *Whos*!

YES ☐ NO ☐